Japa Fire

Africa Migration Report Poetry Anthology Series

Japa Fire
An Anthology of Poems on African and African Diasporic Migration

Edited by Ambrose Musiyiwa and Munya R

First published in Great Britain in 2024 by
CivicLeicester
y. https://www.youtube.com/user/CivicLeicester
f. https://www.facebook.com/CivicLeicester
CivicLeicester@gmail.com

ISBN-13: 978-1-9164593-9-7

© Copyright for individual poems rests with the authors
© Anthology selection copyright: Ambrose Musiyiwa and Munya R
Cover image: "Fire in Close Up Photography" © Jan van der Wolf

The rights of the authors have been asserted in accordance with the UK Copyright, Designs and Patents Act 1988.

All rights are reserved. Except for the quotation of short passages for the purpose of criticism and review, no part of this publication may be reproduced, stored in or introduced into a retrieval system or transmitted in any form or by any means (electronic, mechanical, photocopying, recording or otherwise) without written permission of the publisher.

This book is sold subject to the condition that it shall not, by way of trade or otherwise, be lent, resold, hired out or otherwise circulated without the publisher's prior consent in any form of binding or cover other than that in which it is published and without a similar condition including this condition being imposed on the subsequent purchaser.

The publisher has used its best endeavours to ensure that the URLs for external websites referred to in this book are correct and active at the time of going to press. However, the publisher has no responsibility for the websites and make no guarantee that a site will remain live or that the content is or will remain appropriate.

Every effort has been made to trace all copyright holders, but if any have been inadvertently overlooked, the publisher will be pleased to include any necessary credits in any subsequent reprint or edition.

Dedicated to all who are looking for a better life.

CONTENTS

	Introduction	ix
1	*Horizon* Abíọ́dún Abdul	1
2	*Statuesque* Abíọ́dún Abdul	3
3	*Èrò Ọkọ̀ Àṣìrí – Secret Passenger* Abíọ́dún Abdul	5
4	*The Proud Afrikan* Nzingha Assata	7
5	*I'm Saying That I Am Afrikan* Nzingha Assata	8
6	*Over the Horizon* Nzingha Assata	9
7	*The Japa Fire* Ayo Ayoola-Amale	10
8	*Refugees* Ayo Ayoola-Amale	11
9	*The Last Refugee* Ayo Ayoola-Amale	12
10	*Tall Trees Burn More Wood* Jo Blackwood	13
11	*Culturally* Jo Blackwood	17
12	*eyes open wide* Jo Blackwood	18
13	*Small Mercies* Efua Boadu	19
14	*Okukor* Efua Boadu	20
15	*The Promised Land* Efua Boadu	22
16	*DayStar (39)* Efua Boadu	23
17	*Submerged in The South* Anayo Dioha	24
18	*Panegyric of an African poetry anthology* Anayo Dioha	25
19	*Surviving Japa* Anayo Dioha	27
20	*Ode to the Four Market Days* Anayo Dioha	28
21	*Black and Privileged* Philippa Hatendi-Louiceus	29

22	*The Knives' Symphony* Philippa Hatendi-Louiceus	30
23	*The Hand* Philippa Hatendi-Louiceus	31
24	*Notes for a chronology of smell* Amanda Holiday	32
25	*Poem for Nesyamun* Amanda Holiday	33
26	*A Whiff of Something* Amanda Holiday	34
27	*African Icarus* Amanda Holiday	35
28	*Forgotten Voices* Sello Huma	37
29	*An Ode to Makeba* Sello Huma	38
30	*The Crossroads Spirits of the Dead Migrants Must Return Home* Sello Huma	39
31	*Africa 2063* Sello Huma	40
32	*The Dance* Nandi Jola	41
33	*Dear Belgium* Nandi Jola	42
34	*The Great Migration* Nandi Jola	43
35	*The Toppling of a Statue* Nandi Jola	44
36	*Direction of* Ilan Kelman	45
37	*You To Prorogue In Absentia* Ilan Kelman	46
38	*From Away to Home* Ilan Kelman	47
39	*West Africa and the Middle East* Tifany MarSah	48
40	*Ode to red cedar wooden furniture* Tifany MarSah	50
41	*The Machine* Tifany MarSah	52
42	*On The Move* Epiphanie Mukasano	54
43	*Voyage of Freedom* M Sahr Nouwah	56
44	*Global Citizen* M Sahr Nouwah	58

45	*Migrant Promenade* M Sahr Nouwah	60
46	*I'm ~~not~~ home* Mark Kennedy Nsereko	62
47	*The Color Trials* Mark Kennedy Nsereko	63
48	*In Kakuma* Mark Kennedy Nsereko	64
49	*In Utopia* Mark Kennedy Nsereko	65
50	*Lost in Despair* Collins Chibunna Nwachukwu	66
51	*Forced Marriage* Collins Chibunna Nwachukwu	68
52	*Let Pan-Africanism Lead* Collins Chibunna Nwachukwu	70
53	*Knotted Bodies of Water* Helidah Ogude-Chambert	71
54	*Strange Fish* Helidah Ogude-Chambert	72
55	*Searching for the Gap* Omobola Osamor	73
56	*Following the Ancestor's Map to Freedom* Omobola Osamor	75
57	*Home is* Omobola Osamor	77
58	*Man hours* Adaora Raji	78
59	*Mirror mirror on the wall* Adaora Raji	79
60	*we go where the grass is greener and the oceans are bluest* Adaora Raji	81
61	*Fugitives of the Sun* Laurène Southe	82
62	*Untitled* Laurène Southe	83
63	*Mundele* Laurène Southe	84
	Contributors	85
	Acknowledgements	89
	Organisers	91
	Financial Support	92

INTRODUCTION

Japa Fire: An Anthology of Poems on African and African Diasporic Migration is the first in a new series of poetry anthologies exploring themes around African and African diasporic migration and (im)mobility, the Africa Migration Report Poetry Anthology Series.

Organised by Forced Migration and The Arts in collaboration with CivicLeicester and Regularise, the series draws inspiration from the second edition of the *Africa Migration Report* (African Union Commission and the International Organization for Migration, 2024).[1]

The series differs from the AUC/IOM report in that while the latter is a formal report, the former explores multifaceted narratives on African and African diasporic migration and (im)mobility through poetry, and offers personal, familial and community histories, memories, experiences, hopes, dreams and aspirations around African and African diasporic migration and mobility.

Japa Fire: An Anthology of Poems on African and African Diasporic Migration takes its title from "The Japa Fire", a poem by Ayo Ayoola-Amale exploring Nigerian experiences of irregular migration. The collection features 63 poems from 20 poets, some with many poetry collections and titles to their name, alongside others who are appearing in print for the first time through this anthology. Each poem has been selected for how it speaks to themes around African and African diasporic migration and (im)mobility, and to other poems in the collection, and for how each contributes to the conversation taking place around the world on the themes.

In presenting 63 poems from 20 poets, we are riffing off the African Union's *Agenda 2063: The Africa We Want*[2] as part of efforts to draw attention to The Agenda. We encourage readers and writers alike – and all who have an interest in the continent and its pasts, presents and futures – to read and engage with both the *Africa Migration Report* (AUC and IOM, 2024) and *Agenda 2063*.

We also invite poets to be unfettered in imagining and envisaging possible and better futures for Africans on the continent, in the diaspora and on the move. And we invite similar levels of attention to be paid to those living in formal and informal refugee camps and settlements, in ghettos and slums, on the streets, in prisons, detention centres and other hostile environments, and in cities, towns and villages on the continent and around the world.

---

[1] African Union (2024). Press Release. Africa Migration Report: Linking policy, practice and the welfare of the African migrant Internal: Africa Migration Report. African Union, 26 March. Available at: https://au.int/en/pressreleases/20240326/africa-migration-report-linking-policy-practice-and-welfare-african-migrant [Accessed: 19 October 2024]

[2] https://au.int/en/agenda2063/overview

With both *Japa Fire* and subsequent collections in the Africa Migration Report Poetry Anthology Series, we call for a world in which the rights of African migrants are respected and protected, and in which freedom of movement extends to and includes Africans on the continent, in the diaspora and on the move. And we encourage Africans on the continent, in the diaspora and on the move to meet more and connect with each other more, and talk to and support and collaborate with each other more.

As explained in the AUC and IOM's *Africa Migration Report: 2nd Edition*, states on the African continent are currently working towards setting up a free movement infrastructure better than that which is in place in the European Union.

We hope *Japa Fire* and the Africa Migration Report Poetry Anthology Series will encourage African countries to pick up the pace on the plans, and ensure that freedom of movement is a right that Africans on the continent, in the diaspora and on the move can enjoy alongside all the rights identified in the African Charter on Human and People's Rights. These include the right to freedom from discrimination (Articles 2 and 18(3)); freedom from cruel, inhuman and degrading treatment and punishment (Article 5); the right to life and personal integrity (Article 4), and the right to dignity (Article 5) – all of which are routinely violated by state and non-state actors alike in their treatment of Africans on the continent, in the diaspora and on the move.

And we hope the poetry and readings and conversations that will flow from it will encourage Africans on the continent, in the diaspora and on the move to participate actively in the dialogue that is taking place on the continent and in the diaspora on this.

Ambrose Musiyiwa and Munya R,
England, December 2024

Abíọ́dún Abdul
Horizon

I was born in this foreign land,
My home lies south across the seas
Across the dry Sahara sands
There's a land that holds my first family.

A land of warmth, a land of love,
So many thousands of miles away
And I know when the time is right
I'll go back there to die one day.

But there was a time when I was unsure
If I ever want to return to my home
After all it was this foreign land
Throughout my life that I had known –

It was here I took my first step,
Grew my first tooth, said my first word –
It was in this place I learned all that I knew
It was also in this place I first heard

Racism, a term alien to me
A compulsion I truly did not understand
It was from that point I began to realise
My life would not go as my innocence had planned

I hated the darkness which engulfed my skin
As did those around me who cringed at the sight
I only ever wanted to be treated the same
So for this obligation, I had to fight.

And through my fight – I lost my pain
As I began to see through all my rage
Something very dear which I almost lost
The spirits of my fathers and my heritage

With this in mind, it became clear
Whatever rainbow colour you and I might be
We all have good and we all have bad
This system is called humanity
This system helps to cure disease
And this system caused the two great wars

When hate is in control, it brings pain
So I have learned to love as I have never before.

The past inspired this knowledge in me
And I hope to take it very far
I'll teach it to children all across the world
Before I join my first family: the Yorùbá.

Abíọ́dún Abdul
Statuesque

Distant traveller homecoming on Yorùbá shores,
Èkó evenings bring pub quiz family fun
Only I know the answer to 'wasabi' queries –
Bringing laughter and smiles from east to west

Wandering from event space mirth,
Heading for adjacent mirrored chambers
A statue bust plays welcoming foyer host,
Wrapped in golden Benin regality

'Oh, what high cheek bones you have!' I exalt
'Oh, what rounded nose curves you have!' I gush
'Oh, what protruding full lips you have!' I praise
What unique features piercing my virgin eyes

Nomadic traveller navigating global routes,
Many a statute have passed me by
From Roman 'pretty' posers to Xian's warrior soldiers;
Stone-works chiselled in my asymmetric reflection, the 'norm'

This Gleaming Monarch before me hits different,
and tourist conditioning demands a selfie!
Smiling wide as camera flashes glint gold,
Time to inspect 2D snaps of 3D memory

'Ah … your High Cheek Bones … are mine(!)'
'Yet … your Rounded Nose Curves … is me(!)'
'But … your Protruding Full Lips … be I(!)'
My symmetric reflection majestically moulded

Fixated traveller in stock-still disorientation,
eyes dancing upon the pixelated rendering
Absorbing intricate art imitating *my* life
Humanity's proto/phenotype: melanated African

My God-sculpted familiar features 'unique'?
A cognitive query I knew not the answer for
I face trusted mirrors everyday, surveying my beloved norm
But cast into metallic or stone eternity heralded thrilling innovation

Gone too far, too long, too young from Yorùbá shores;

a global wanderer now shaking off 'foreign' eyes
New laughter and smiles for this: my statuesque celebration
Grateful to hold court with stoic Benin Brethren

Abíọ́dún Abdul
Èrò Ọkọ̀ Àṣìrí – Secret Passenger

Riding life's journey on this London train
Stoic glass panes exposing the sprawling global village
This empty compartment housing my lone silhouette
Embarking on my true destination: meeting family, friendship, delight
Wheelsets soundly spinning towards smiles, hugs and Yorùbá greetings

Linguistic isolation whilst stationed north
Familial interactions compartmentalised within Èdèkiri code
Changing semantic tracks within one household
Melding English A, B, C with Yorùbá tonal do, ray, mi
Family knowledge embedded in secret lexical and grammatical melodies

These word platforms bonding Yorùbá mothers, daughters, sisters near
These communication carriages connecting Yorùbá aunties, nieces, cousins far
Now stationed south, closer to Èdèkiri codebreakers beyond family circles
I head towards an opus of fun dialogues and cultural exploration
Vocal toot-tooting, basking in community and identity ... chugga chug faster ọkọ̀ ojú irin a.k.a. train!

Riding life's journey on this London train
Impending reunion excitement meets freshly evoked curiosity
A melanated family quintette joins my secret compartment, filling blue vinyl seats
The whooshing winds now supporting their vivacious voices sharing compartmentalised truths
Family mirth, workplace triumphs, neighbour botheration ... in my secret language!

These unperceptive Èdèkiri encoders talk freely in my presence
Their stimulating tales evoke a stationary dance behind my eyes
A passive passenger in their dynamic Yorùbá vehicle.
As they stir life conversations in different directions, diverse and divergent
My bilingual brain joins this free incidental road trip navigating new life pathways

Eagerly eavesdropping in plain sight on my oblivious trustees
To remain perceptive, I remain receptive ... but almost stamp my own ticket
With a glance ... then a look ... then staring back and forth at my lingual artistes

A smiling Ìyá-aged lady meets my wandering gaze, her own silent thoughts booming,
'Aa-aa, ṣé "Ará Gẹ̀ẹ́sì" yi gbọ́ wa?' a.k.a. 'Ah, does this "Brit" understand us?'

Commandeering life's journey on this London train
I am indeed a silent passenger in their business, a linguistic stowaway
Syntax pickpocket, semantics robber, knowledge thief of 'stolen' banter.
A privacy fare dodger intent on evading capture, I avert unsmiling eyes
Adorning a mask of 'unrecognition', greedy for more attention from my mother tongue

More Yorùbá musicality flows from my personal quintette of trained concert conductors
Ear satellites scanning for more coverage from mouths tuned with tonal precision
My performative tone deafness to these everyday rhythm of life lyrics now more convincing
Muting my gaze to stay on track for more announcements in my secret lexis with 55 million+ speakers yonder
Granted through exclusionary hubris, fortified with perceived Èdè Gẹ̀ẹ́sì language barriers

Págà! My Èdèkiri FM easy listening derailed as brakes slow our locomotion
For once, why did a London train have to fulfil its timetabled arrival?
I decompartmentalise as I disembark, heading towards my original Yorùbá familial destination
Happy for this unwitting warm up act beforehand, and wider accessibility in the global village
A joyous train of thought reaching the end of the line for this èrò ọkọ̀ àṣìrí a.k.a. secret passenger

Nzingha Assata
The Proud Afrikan

One day I looked within and saw someone else
Not myself as I was or used to be but a new self
A self that travelled back in time to a far off past in a distant land
A land which I knew not and there I saw in the distance
The agonised faces of my brothers and sisters
The chains had been loosened but the scars remained
Deep in the minds and hearts of the proud Afrikan
My spirit sank my mind recoiled from the cruel reality
Of the enslavement of Afrikans
Could this evil really have happened I thought aloud
No one answered me

And so, my mind, as it raced through time, was filled with dread
Because of the horror and anguish there before me daring me to open
My mind to the truth of what was done to the proud Afrikan
Our ancestors tried so hard to be brave and strong
And I can feel within me their spirit
As I behold the lash upon their backs, scarring them for life
Could this be true I asked myself that human beings carried out this evil
This shameful cruel abuse and terror and nearly destroyed
The Proud Afrikan.

Who did this evil to us Afrikans, I asked
From somewhere far off in the distance came the reply
Fellow human beings destroyed used and abused the proud Afrikan
As I looked my eyes enlarged the horror came nearer and nearer
Threatening to engulf me in a sea of unreality
I must get back I cried back to my world of safety
Too late, too late, said the voice of the proud Afrikan
I didn't blink as I recognised the crease of pain upon their brow
And felt my heart break that they should have suffered
Such shame and torment for the Arab and the white man's greed
Time has moved on but still today they are here still oppressing the proud
    Afrikan
So, people don't expect me to smile or laugh at your crude jokes and
    insensitivity
For they touch the hearts of me and mine
For we bear the scars of the proud Afrikan

Nzingha Assata
I'm Saying That I Am Afrikan

When you see me
Socially, politically, ideologically
I'm saying loudly that I am Afrikan
When you see me and I'm making a fuss
Or just having a cuss
It is because I have been denied the right for many, many, years
To publicly recognise
That I am Afrikan
When you see me walking along the streets
If I ignore you sister, brother
Don't take offence, hail me
For I wouldn't wilfully pass you by
But you see my mind is now full up
Of the reality of my misery as I struggle to analyse
How to make Europeans pay for destroying us Afrikans

My whole being now as a conscious woman
Must pave the way and set the scene
For other young women to embrace Afrikaness
For when the chains of slave mentality roll away
You awake to find that you are somebody
You awake to find Afrikan pride
You awake to find you are a human being
You awake to consciousness
And your responsibility to expose those who have kept you in bondage
So, come Afrikan sisters, brothers
Reaffirm your right to be not a slave
Not a negro, not a Black
Reaffirm your right to be known as Afrikan

Nzingha Assata
Over the Horizon

My eyes can see clearly over the horizon
To the day when my offspring
Will return to the land of our fore-parents
To the day when Afrikans will no longer relish
Enslavement in other people's land

My eyes look longingly across the waters
To see how far away the day of Afrikan freedom is
My blood stirs as I realise with unshed tears in my eyes
That we are nearing that day
For our slavery has been overlong but we are now becoming strong
And all the world will see
We will no longer be taken advantage of
Freedom must come
For Afrika and Afrikans
And Afrikans must be freed
Freed from greed and destruction
Freed from the contamination of Arab and European greed and destruction

Ayo Ayoola-Amale
The Japa Fire

Once upon the same old story
about me, about others
yesterday
even this morning.
My papa didn't give me a name;
I was told 'The soul has neither tribe nor colour'
I was told 'The soul needs no travel permit
sandwiched between the sun and the moon.'
And so, my name is humankind
I am the flower by the river
full of legs, all native.
The earth makes love, then seeds
sing,
and fill the tireless land.
All I have, all I got, I gather
to journey
in a handicap boat crowded like an old graveyard
I, a frail weed stem fell asleep,
Then a part of me fell into the ocean; a stream
of light cracked, dropping straight on my floating backpack
everyone screaming, crying not screaming, were barely alive.
Then I became the hospital corridor,
wrapped up, shrunken
crumbling
in the 'Japa sickness'
convulsing
me trying to flee 'Sapa life' to buy a space on a river
of money.' Me running away from the buttons of 'Wahala'
on a hospital bench, staring at rooftops.
'Japa' poured fire
on my burnt-out places
sat on my head, with such force
that anger painted a deep
gorge hung everywhere.
a mind – gunned, a stray plank –
the sounds of breaths collapsing.

Japa means 'to run' or 'to flee'
Sapa (/sa:kpa/) means a state of financial incapacity or extreme poverty.
Wahala means problem, suffering

Ayo Ayoola-Amale
Refugees

We saw our buildings boiling hot,
we saw our roads screaming
our souls found the wings to fly upon the storm.
Our homes are the doorway of fire shattering our villages
in the cover of gloom.
Not one person knows our pain,
They see our legs fly everywhere
They see our souls drowning
and our horrified ancestors fleeing
then they smash the bridges and
go to sleep.

Ayo Ayoola-Amale
The Last Refugee

My coat saw me off farther peeking out at my foot,
I woke taking the bit of soil with its breath into my eyes

Then I fell asleep sucking my mum's breast –

this place welcomes me at twenty-one, as the night was in labour
I'd jumped on a kite between the mountain's thick forest –

the desert where the ocean covers up spirits.
My lineage is not there in my lineage

like the flower separated from the stem step by step,
I became the chick the hawk stole from the hen

then the hen vanishes into the hawk

holding on to a dream as the morning ripens.

Jo Blackwood
Tall Trees Burn More Wood

Tall trees burn more wood
And the ashes have scattered
Many have picked up the batten
Because it still matters
Maybe not the same pain but then again we still strive for our own
    Promised Land

Some turning points in history
Depending how you interpret the movement from the 1960s
I feel the journey has come far
Though my humanness blurs my perspective – centuries of repression
– What else would it do but leave scars?

Tall trees
Can I really talk about the scenes from the past 50 years?
About all the things that helped toughen my hide
Through things that stole their pride and – for more than short moments –
    made them cry

Can I actually contrast them days to now?
Could I live in those times with the fear of someone wanting to blow up my
    behind for expressing these sensitive lines?
Makes me feel real grateful to be right here and right now
But would all mankind agree?
'Cos ain't there still life situations fraught with pain and desolation, war
    without cessation and unseen misery?

Still, I have to figure a place
How do I make a difference?
It's easy for the words to slip from these lips
But how do I answer that question that's demanding like a lonely child,
    silently begging for affection?
However I make a difference it has to be major and not mild – I need to pay
    attention!

In comparison to the days of Martin Luther King
My stuff seems trivial – I shouldn't have no complaints
While he worked for a promised land reality
I may encounter closed off gates
Making me feel I've come too late
See eyes that don't hide hate

But we all in the same race!
Our humanness is a collective thing that won't outdate

Dr King shared his feelings despite – as a consequence he died
His loving words unsettled the few that cut short his fight and his life!
Did he declare like Maya Angelou, "And Still I Rise"?
The gift of life now I see as a prize

>   Tall trees burn too
>   He threw the change into my leathered palm
>   Avoiding any physical contact
>   I recognized the fear –
>   I got that
>   But my epidermis was covered from the tips to my exposed wrists
>   I was wearing gloves
>   – he wouldn't have got an illness if he had touched this

Whatever skin you're lingering in
We all have the same workings of scabs seeping blood
The same pain – the same hidden strains
In all dimensions
It just feels like nobody else does

>   Tall trees burn more wood
>   In this time of recession
>   Big change, funding and job cuts
>   I see scores of people enjoying their living during this 'credit
>   crunch'
>   Even if a little part of themselves is cut off
>   The worry and the wrath hidden behind designer cloths
>   A myriad of powerful sensations – opposite to peace
>   That constantly need regulating – like the police
>
>   I struggle sometimes to see through unfinished tasks
>   – for perfection
>   Do you sometimes feel the pressure
>   – like somehow you weren't ready for this selection?
>   And we're not even amongst the masses that are weary of
>   premature death
>   Through the KKK and that type of stuff
>   'Cos they don't stand up to measure
>   Their life already delicate like a feather

Tall trees stand
Strived to put on a plain mask

To look a certain way AND feel relaxed
Searching for acceptance outside of myself
But now
When deep-seated grins mixed with sparkling eyes are returned back
It breaks me into a laugh – and I love focusing on that!

Tall trees burn
I didn't want to moan about the state of the world
Constantly bombarded with images that aren't you or me
I don't want to preach. I do that naturally!
I want to say I'm for the sighting of hurdles being cleared
Like a World Record breaking Jamaican sprinter
Accelerating with more than 5 gears

    Tall trees stand
    Hand in hand
    Forgetting the backstreets
    Expressing affection

    It's dark, a little breezy
    He is wearing his hoody
    Not to disguise the unsavoury
    But to the slow moving generation this can provoke real tension

    But his hand is in mine
    And we steady, like a slow moving train!
    Our gazes concentrated, fixated
    – I have to look away

    But did he see the fear on their faces
    Maybe his strong disposition meant he wouldn't have cared
    Or does he hide those moments it hurt too much for him to share?
    A tall tree stands

And a tall tree burnt

Dr Martin Luther King
A by-product of your selfless works
– affected change
Like relentless ripples on a lake
You stood for your beliefs when the authorities wouldn't protect
You convinced a whole heap of faces, from all kinds of different places
To combine, causing great effect
Teaching loving changes

Not hiding the behaviour that was unsacred
Your dreams in embryonic stages at the time of your demise

Is this what you wanted to see with your own coloured eyes?
Love without disguise
No strings tied
All merging to feed
Flowing to the same stream

Is this a part of your prophecy a part of your "I Have a Dream" speech?
You a tall tree
A tree that stood

Tall trees burn more wood

Jo Blackwood
Culturally

Culturally
I'm well-adorned

Culturally
also misinformed
adorned with all but my fine African linen
but you see jewellery will not give me a better she
and cars and things will not give him a better he
It's our time to find what's laid behind are opened and closed minds
Take off the limits that restrict my potency to become a supreme being that
keeps me shy
away from my divinity
use word and scriptures quoted to formulate a lighter picture
where dreams come true and desires remain new
a nurturing of the inner soul
to fill the gap logic like a Kit Kat just enough to fill the (w)hole
this is the plan from Source
no one can change what the Source has planned for me to be
and no one can change the path
it's just a matter of time before I allow it into reality

Jo Blackwood
eyes open wide

here and overseas
we see inescapable tragic scenes
scenes of authorised death
masses though
hold their breath in unity
spawning global protests
and the need for solace to refresh in rest

we unify as our inconceivable power is accessed
to further manifest

eyes open wide last night
couldn't synchronise
I couldn't write
aware of scenes giving up worthiness for another's delight
human rights are not confined to one community
nor one skin
we are full of the same haemoglobin that carries the oxygen
earth   hue
we are regal
life is free
there shouldn't be a separate banner proclaiming the darker tones'
right to live freely   fully
breathe
this should be automatic
currently the climate as a whole repeats "it is what it is" pandemic
I get it but I am not applying that refrain to this
cease and desist
the unspoken decline in value of darker skin
it needs to shift
a tangible meaningful change towards inclusion
it is in our palms to act to uplift in richness not in thrift
a movement no covert rules no censorship
for richness are our legacies

Efua Boadu
Small Mercies

No.
I'll not rest
on your old armchair
turned towards the rosary-laden image
of Pope John Paul
left hanging on a cracked blue-brilliant wall
in the compound once called home.
not home. but abroad.
not abroad but home
to my black skin that basked
on a wicker mat used to dry red beans,
collect cassava
that did not dry but lay beside me.
Cassava leaves. Cassava roots.

Cassava that was not to be eaten
but sold by the roadside
leading to the airport that took me
not home, but far away
from that sacred picture frame
draped in blood-red beads
that swayed occasionally
yet remained firm.
unlike me.

I genuflect before John Paul,
feigning reverence, reflecting
on how you used to kiss
the black cross and wish me –
Godspeed.

Efua Boadu
Okukor

Glass encased in a hall,
the statue's beak appears
to droop forlornly.
So far away from home, I sigh.

If it could, I guess it would
ponder on a distant past
when once it crowed
as dawn entered the courtyard.

Wings back, head high,
Okukor would heave
his crimson hackles
and stride haughty

across the clearing.
His weight, a perfect balance
on thin hind shanks,
red crown fluttering,

there was a breeze that day.
The day the Oba's artisan
began to model Okukor
using his fine metal comb.

The artisan's eyes sketched
elegant tail plumes
that seemed to glow
turquoise, gold and blue.

Okukor stopped pecking
and raised his head
as though looking for his hens,
careful to remain in profile.

He relaxed,
moved less cautiously,
stretched his wings wide,
letting the light soak his down,

Okukor knew his worth.
He even remained silent
when later the axe pierced
his neck for royal sacrifice.

But this was not the end.

For, in the beginning,
Oduduwa, the divine king
descended from the heavens
carrying Okukor under his arm.

The cock's beak scratched
and pecked the Earth
to forge the hills and valleys
of the sixteen kingdoms.

Creator.
Mythmaker.
Okukor – Cambridge
will never tame you.

Efua Boadu
The Promised Land

Piccadilly Gardens
saturated with spice heads
ket, blow, Asmarinos
for Just Eat & Deliveroo,
asylum application woes.
Headwind to Massawa or
foot of the Hindu Kush –
how did they sail the route?
      When a few are gathered
they anoint a remembrancer
who mutters memories interred:
lest they forget Agadez,
once sanctuary to Hajjis,
now strangers trade their wares
or their bodies, or both, on the way to Tripoli,
then to Italy, inshallah.
The elders, choked in sea-blue tagelmust,
warned the youngers, 'don't forget your past,'
but witnessing the ribs of a goatherd
protrude then snap like cinders
survival mouldered to dust.
      Time to go.
The boys' pickup staggered
along the ancient caravan route
strewn with cattle skulls.
Bartered black bodies sold
like Amazigh rugs, fat-tailed sheep,
it's 2016: you cannot extinguish smoke
ravenous for the cliffs.
It's Cousin Ali's fault,
he assured them Europe
was sleeping like Mara's baby.
'I could never do that,' a Naija girl told me,
Her best friend is in Sicily. In the profile
she's smiling, but the length of skirt,
sheer crop top,
are dried roses in too much heat.
Don't think: focus on the heft of the tyres,
the thickness of the bike frame.
His fresh face, but the hands are wrinkled.
Efua Boadu

DayStar (39)
To the 39 Vietnamese people who died in October 2019 in Grays, Essex after being smuggled to the UK in the back of a lorry.

as to a lamp shining in a dark place:
behold a vision upon a holy mountain.
A light at the end of a tunnel, that never came
(and you were doing well in paying attention to it).

Behold a vision upon a holy mountain.
It never came,
yet, still the day dawned and embraced you all
(and you were doing well in paying attention to it)

it never came
that daylight, trapped at the end of a tunnel
(and you were doing well in paying attention to it);
endlessly awaiting the dawn to never be

that daylight, trapped at the end of a tunnel,
as to a lamp shining in a dark place:
endlessly awaiting the dawn to never be
a light. At the end of a tunnel. It never came.

Anayo Dioha
Submerged in The South

I can see you brother. Hope you
remember me at the sight of this.
I can see you from down here,
my voice too unloud to travel
through the distance that demarcates
my lips from your ears; down here
where dirt and debris are all I have
for bed and breakfast while you snooze
ahead in lust and lavishness; down here
with my young blood in my arms
bleeding away the shackles of a dream
life before an ER in dire need of an ER,
as a Swiss surgeon jets in at your fingers'
snap bearing painkillers for your fingertips;
down here where savage Sahara yawns
with glistening glare and sword-sharp
appetite at my torn torso and the
blood-drunk Mediterranean growls
as the fading shadow of my hope awaits
my most uncertain arrival at Lampedusa,
while up there, first-hosted, you toast
to safe skies, clanging glasses
of what savoury delight champagne or
wherever-the-heck-else's got to offer.
I can see you brother, down here.
Hope you see me too.

Anayo Dioha
Panegyric of an African poetry anthology

I had always been in awe of that word.
Anthology. I must have looked it up
a number of times. To get to know it better,
of course. But we never seemed to have
been fully familiarised with each other.
All fairness to it, something about it always
comes off distinct. I mean, it sort of doesn't
share from the commonality of journals,
mags, contemporaries of the sort.

Who knew that time had a better plan
towards a grander meeting? Who would
have thought the gods of my ancestors
had prepared me for lunch and dinner
with my most enchanted literary word,
where I would be an honoured guest,
sharing the table with honoured poets?
And when it came, it came with a bang,
a splash and some ripples, ushering me
into a warm reception like we had known
each other from the deepest memory
of time, never requiring of me a strenuous
schooling to engage with the demands
of its themed event; so home I was I
could even contribute my voice from
the depths of dozing. Now, I don't have

to go into a duel with anxiety to tell
the tales from my soil — how decadence
and dearth drive my kinspeople to distant
tents across the ocean; how distance
assumes their chief architect of asunder;
how bellies are filled like balloons, but
not with air but with salt water, yet more
and more hearts sail, undaunted seemingly,
but innately fuelled by elusive hope; how,
most dishearteningly, the keepers at my
neighbour's gate shut the door in my face
and turned their backs at me, when all
I sought was to know them better and
work together to actualise a richer home

soil, which made me wonder if they truly
took time to consider the Charter. Now,

I don't mean that global Charter, no.
I mean our Charter, the one that directs,
among many directions, that our doors
must not be shut in neighbours' faces.

Anayo Dioha
Surviving Japa

She is royal and beautiful,
Like the affluent evergreens
Of this wetland under West African
Pre-dusk, as the squirrels squeak
And the crickets chirp
And gold adorns the sky.

She is royal and priceless,
Pitched to me by the least expected
Soulmate agents: a kinsman of mine and
His wife, her cuz. We became a ship
From the Port of Acquaintance.
I'm saturated by her voice,
Like fire fills a pot with steam.

She leaves as others leave, for a greener view
– Caught in the exodus epidemic – the Japa Flu.
From across Niagara Falls,
She reaches me, the smart screen
Our veritable vaccine variant.

She Skypes me on the exploits
Of winter and summer and WhatsApps
On the demands of campus professors
For her preferred pronouns.
I'm positive we'll conquer the perils
Of the Distance Sea and dock
Safely at the Port of Reunion.

Anayo Dioha
Ode to the Four Market Days

Like seasons through a western year do dance,
You bring sweet colour to my weekly days:

Spring, Summer, Autumn, Winter;
Eke, Orie, Afọ, Nkwọ!

Philippa Hatendi-Louiceus
Black and Privileged

All I do is cross borders.
I have no desire to integrate or to belong,
I don't need a new life.
I know who I am.
Better, for me, was always where everyone looked like me.
I am black and privileged.
Half of nothing, wholly African.
Wholly royal. Proud.
Free to move as I please.
No patchwork identity, no struggle with self.
My ancestors have sat right in front of me my whole life,
On my shoulder like angels waiting with me at every port.
I am not struggling. I have never scrounged for scraps.
My growing pains were yours.
I have never been less than anybody. I never will be.
Starting again was never a dying necessity,
But it is the only thing that makes me feel like I am part of the world.
That I could pick up my whole life in a bag and start again.
I am transient. Constantly transitioning.
Black passports always seem to be the things that people are trying to shed.
What makes their life hard,
To be from one of those places whose flag swims in black faces.
It's the reason why they have to wait for hours in the baking heat in
    embassy lines,
Or are half-dead with thirst on a boat somewhere in the sea.
Black faces always need scars to be worthy of attention.
They need empty bellies drenched in poverty porn and unsurmountable
    odds.
Fighting spirit and a desire to survive.
Heroism derived from lack, from scrambling, from rejection.
I am not the story with a black face that everyone wants to tell.
All I acknowledge is black joy.
There are many faces like mine,
But no place for our stories.

Philippa Hatendi-Louiceus
The Knives' Symphony

They used broken knives to make music
Hollowed out carved wood so it would echo
Through the bamboo trees that had found themselves in this land.
Imported,
Just like them.
Not native, but home
Made a home
You may wonder
Why knives?
They don't make music.
Only pain,
Only loss,
The mothers of wounds.
But you forget,
They take what's from the ground
What's from the trees,
With their sharp edges and tips
Break it down,
Cleeve and carve it,
So we may nourish ourselves
And our little ones.
Women pass with sturdy, metal pots filled with these broken morsels,
Heavy with steel, licked hot by flames.
A hot pot can never burn our black mothers' fingers
And those fingers hold the knives that sustain us all.
Though knives have been held here by native hands,
For terror,
For pain,
For death,
The fathers of suffering.
They have also made music,
Music bound in the ancestors' proverbs
Ayibobo
That brings us back to ourselves,
Under the bruised setting sun,
The sanguine sea air in the trees.

Philippa Hatendi-Louiceus
The Hand

I fell in love.
With a nation.
When I was new to the world and filled with the optimism of youth.
Filled with that blind sunlight that leads you to believe everything will be alright.
Only if we can value. Only if we could value ourselves more.
The sunshine at the beach exploded inside me while I sipped my rhum sour, and smiled. Smiled at the dark-skinned, dark-haired, light-filled boy on the beach. The boy who had been looking at me while pretending he wasn't.
Pretending shyness. Pretending nothing. Pretending all.
The streets where I danced, danced behind the carnival trucks in the throng of black bodies just like mine jostling with the inscrutable thrum of life.
Shorts too short.
Curves too curvy.
In a culture that was always on display – on TV screens, radios and statuses. Always too loud, always too vibrant, too many colours surging forward and melting into violence.
Melting into violence.
In those same streets where our feet danced, we have descended into violence.
The feet that cascade on the pavement are running from the gunfire in the air.
Running with everything they can carry, with their babies and the things they used to make a home. Now we must learn to make homes, homes again with only the things we can carry.
The boys we danced with now hold guns in our faces.
In the faces of our children.
Hold a nation hostage.
Some say it's the heat. Some say we got too much sun. Some say it's the loa sitting too hot in our heads.
Some say it's the hand that's always meddling, but I say what happens when that hand is you?
That hand is you.

Amanda Holiday
Notes for a chronology of smell

vernix sweat cheese / stuff of life
dank begins / skin smeared birth

sakitomboy pepper-mash mackerel
silver sting cooks / palm street pan

chewing gum powder /light sweet
silver foil-wrap hidden car nook

alphabet biscuits, oven vanilla warm
almond-heat shortbread/ guests due

red rubric earth, salty tar ashy soil
cheetahs dash shapes floodlit

woman dances on stage / turns
into paper strips / burns to ash

butter-white breakfast bread
rolls Elder Dempster ship

grey Chorley rain stains
pavements to coal

Amanda Holiday
Poem for Nesyamun

'Bed/bad'
the voice of Nesyamun
glottal frogged otherworldly
uttering 3000 years wayback
'bed/bad bed bād bĕd bad bed'
bitter tobacco bleat of muted curse
belched vowels blunted by rag and
bone and time and death
a coughed-up gag

'bed bad'
hums the microphone
scientists listen, chilled
Nesyamun speaks at last
no sleeping beauty this
cracked and crooked refugee
crabby on his wake, his bed hard
the sleep too long, the pain
too great.

Amanda Holiday
A Whiff of Something

An artist-poet goes to a party in Hout Bay in Cape Town. The hosts are a white photojournalist and his wife. On the wall in their kitchen is a photograph of the journalist in Rwanda holding a black baby. The poet is struck by the expression on the man's face. On closer inspection, she realises that the infant he holds is dead—there is a bullet hole in the middle of the baby's forehead. The journalist tells them how, when he returned from Rwanda, he had the smell of death in his nose. His wife nods as he speaks. He tries to get the smell out of his nose every morning; he rinses his nostrils out with soap, uses sprays, plunges his nose deep into bouquets of agapanthus. One day his wife tells him the smell is inside his head and he needs to see a doctor. Everyone nods sympathetically.

Amanda Holiday
African Icarus

He fell from the sky
– no one knew who he was
an African Icarus
his head smashed onto the crazy paving
in a Clapham garden
but he was already dead
frostbitten in the wheelwell
of the 787 out of Jomo Kenyatta
international, 2 hours in, the water bottle
untouched along with the bread

His friend knew a friend who knew a man
who had flown for free this way under a turbo jet
to Paris afterdark, cut a hole in the airfield fence
no one saw, ran to the undercar, scaled the iron
bird leg, tucked himself in a corner with just a bag,
damp towel for fumes, cork for his ears,
slugged triple whiskey straight, bit his lip hard,
covered his nose with the cloth
as the thundering tyres pounded the runway
then up and up and up in prayer

Father into your hands I lend my spirit
he willed himself into a trance, they say

He's living large now a Paris, sends money
back western union every month end
His mother is building a house in Nairobi

Thus he dreamed.
He was the skinny kid
with ashy knot knees who
outran the old trains on the platform
at Imara Diama station on Mombasa Road
then one time he jumped the Premier's
car in the street and danced on top
two fingers popping off at all the cheers
until security jumped out and grabbed
him pummelling him to the ground
He nearly died then

His mother was watching the BBC news
idly, ironing for some white lady when they
mentioned Kenya Airways and she
saw a photo of some Indian man some student
in London who had been laid out in his garden
sunbathing. When the body hit from the sky
Right then something in her heart snagged
she grabbed a dress to her nose and smelled
kerosene and then she screamed and screamed
because she knew that damn fool
fell from the plane was her son

Sello Huma
Forgotten Voices

Where I come from, my children are without business partners
like orphans in the investment section
parented by poverty, drugs and witchcraft
betrayed by the unequal uniformed social system
my children hanged with empty taps and high tax
daily soaked and raped by the new puppets
worshipping tenders and IMF lenders under
the parliamentary carpets
targeting service delivery
budgets while the masses eat and sleep with
uncollected toilet buckets
forgotten by fellow comrades
in high walls
even though they sacrificed their lives
on the frontline to free Mandela and the others

Sello Huma
An Ode to Makeba

Thank you for answering the call
to heal the world with music
How can we forget your spiritual
melodies and harmonies of black love and peace
piercing through our ears
We did not dance to forget your message
we danced to live up to the kofifi blues
even though, they called it Jazz
You dished us Marabi, the soul food
of Sophiatown brewed from the townships
and villages
Daughter of Gqwashu, Goddess of the Khoisan
You sacrificed your life for the oppressed
And liberated our souls from the bush
I salute your bravery to free us from mental slavery
Mr Verwoerd could not see what you could see
Even though you were banned from your ancestral land
You shouted black power from across the border with your fists up
The children of Soweto replied from the classrooms
and took the revolution to the streets
You bore all the atrocities with your people on the ground
knowing how it feels like to lose a child as a mother
Tears of the struggles remember your greatness

Sello Huma
The Crossroads Spirits of the Dead Migrants Must Return Home

Remember those who transitioned in crowded rickety vessels sailing to
 Europe
those thousands washed by the waves of the ocean
In search of pounds, dollars and euro signs
Your transitioning lives down a scar full of questions
to the status
quo

Some couldn't face the atomic sounds of bombs and missiles
some tired of corner hunger and poverty
some torn apart by the aftermath of man-made wars
some raped, tortured and sold at the Tripoli Auction market to reach Italy
some are still missing with body parts
and some died in the bundu
swallowed by the crocodile river
some buried alive by heavy thunderstorms of south -west
some are the stones that the builder refused
Those who transitioned in crowded rickety vessels sailing to America
in search of greener pastures
Your spirits must return home to rest
Your spirits must return home for closure
Tell the medicine men to dig up the roots
and throw down the bones
so the spirits can tell us
the kind of sacrifice they desire to return
home
Those crossroads spirits of the dead migrants flowing in the mist
of the Mediterranean Sea
and wandering in the wilderness
must return home to their loved
ones
What about those wailing souls captured by force
during the slave trade who jumped into the Volta for refuge
Their spirits too must be appeased and returned home
Even though we pay homage to you at any crossroads
we
encounter

May your spirits fly and find their way back home someday
so we can live close with the past.

Sello Huma
Africa 2063

Africa will dream the same black dreams
and drink the same black water

Africa will ride on the same black pride
and pray to the same black god

Africa will loosen up the same black fears
and cry the same black tears

Africa will parade the same black sentiments
and demand reparations and justice for black crimes

Africa will speak the same black languages
and wear the same black traditions

Africa will learn from the same black philosophies
and create the same black education

Africa will walk the same black talk
and love with the same black love

Africa will wise up
wake up
rise up
speak up
achieve scientific
technological revolution
economic liberation
total emancipation

Nandi Jola
The Dance

The invitation came handwritten
on ebony paper and in black ink
sealed with red wax
it read six in the evening
a reception at the Manor House:
Wellington Residencies requests the pleasure of your company.

The workers stood by the side entries
peeking from the long, drawn curtains
good evening, Madam,
good evening, gentlemen,
echoing through the gold-lined wallpaper
red carpet, and gold candleholders.

The great painting of the Boer War in the hallway
the opulence of the fresh lilies
by the window
and the dazzling chandeliers
play tricks on the eye
the fireplace; almost sets the tone.

When the lady of the house entered,
Mrs. Wellington,
draped in diamonds,
we all stood in awe
as she dazzled
in the company of her guests.

Let's dance; the Lord exclaimed!

Followed by a trumpet call
foreign fruits
rare meats
on ivory plates
gold goblets
silver cutlery.

Nandi Jola
Dear Belgium

All these years have passed and
you still refuse to open to the world.

How are we to move forward
you and I
in this entanglement of
passports, citizenship, lies, and blood?

Does my dark skin
ring a call in your ears
to look in dark places
of your closets
to see if any skeletons
want a dance with the truth?

Where is your own pride?
Is it buried among the dead?
It can't be in the 180,000 possessions
from Africa
locked up behind the glass
of a display cabinet
that allows you to live in denial.

Nandi Jola
The Great Migration

In a stampede
a baton, a crucifix, and a boot
are the closest things to God.

In Sidi Salem, Nador,
they are digging up mass graves;
God is not there.

In the Moroccan heat
young men crawl on their bellies like snakes,
walls built with fences high —
only the imagination will get them across to the other side.

In a distance tall boats float,
the white sands bring in sardines,
the seagulls' howl —
a far cry from the stampede
and lifeless bodies piling on top of each other.

We will call this the mass immigration.

We will write in our history books that Europe was full.

We will not tell their names.

We will never know their faces.

Nandi Jola
The Toppling of a Statue

The sweet sugar profits that built the lush English countryside
left barren fields
and empty houses in the Caribbean
the Windrush sucked them in
to build England.

Docking in Liverpool
spilling them in factories
young men and women building roads and bridges
for a people that would later tell them
to go back home.

Now these young men and women
who don't belong here
never belonged there
are angrier than the generation before them
where is home to them?

When they looked at Colston's statue
it only reminded them of the sugar
they never got to profit from
a society that never accepted them
no place to really call home.

Rolling him over cobbled streets of Bristol Harbour
over the murky waters
that brought over his wealth
seems like the only glory he deserves

a drowned legacy.

Ilan Kelman
Direction of

Do we know what we seek?
Do we wish what we find?
We are told of new lives.
We are told we'll be free.

It costs so much.
Stress, time, and cash.
In that order.
Who pays, who gains.
In that order.

Reality is now
Risk, yearn, loss, repeat.
Darkness, wetness, chillness, danger.
Emptiness.
Terror, abuse, police, evade.
Hide, hate, hurt, hell.
Where is fullness?
Cannot stop thinking

Thought interlude
We are called Africans.
We are said to come from Africa.
Thousands of ethnicities, thousands of languages.
54 countries, two de facto states, and a confusion of
      exclaves, enclaves
         occupied territories, non-state-actor controlled territories
         islands geologically African, politically European
Does Africa exist as much as hope?
What is this hope of 'Europe'?
Back to reality

Uncontrolled, we arrive
With the promise of a welcome
A promise unfulfilled
Do more evils await?

Trapped in between.
These new lives are worse lives.
What is found is not wished.
We know not what to seek.

Ilan Kelman
You To Prorogue In Absentia

Apocalypse of dreams,
Utopia of nightmares,
The histories of the futures.

The time is arrived
The reasons are lost
The way is onwards

As the bombers take off
Destination unknown.
As the leader's plane explodes
Over hostile territory.
As babies stop an army.
As soldiers lead the peace.

The world shakes
The prismatic pararealities palpitate
        Does gravity
        Does evolution
        Does the double helix
        Does the natural logarithm
        Does the speed of light
        Does the smell of sound
Exist
        or cannot exist.
Superposing, Simulating, Diffracting, Diluting, Refracting, Reflecting
Overlapping, Folding, Flexing, Intermingling, Summing, Multiplying
        each other

Futures from histories
No need for any end

                        (termination)

Ilan Kelman
From Away to Home

Forest was home
Forest was stolen
Logging, farming
Batwa away.
Ogiek away.

New home, new lives
Away from forest
Not home, never home.

Guide tourists to forest
Fight in court for land
Win
Still denied home.

Remember, grieve, remember
Tell knowledge to children
Sing stories to children
Still away, not home.

Sadness with children.
Want joy for children.
Seek home for children.

Forest is home.
Forest land-water-air-life is home.

One day
No more
Away.

Tifany MarSah
West Africa and the Middle East

West Africa and the Middle East can be seen in and on your skin,
The Da Vinci code to your inner being,
Geography in its purest form.
Have you ever wondered who once walked these roads you trace with your
 fingers so gently?
That connect from your dome to the soles of your toes
Lines curved,
and ready to mould,
the taller you grow,
the more creases you will get to show –
West Africa and the Middle East can be seen in and on your skin like the
Topography of the Mountains – they will tell you where you once have
 been,
Only the most high must know why you can find yourself a twin to the
 earth's backbone,
Maybe to show you that your skin isn't actually just skin deep,
Or maybe to show you that taking care of your skin is equally connected to
 the stability within,
Or that the skin-lines you sport can braille all tales of ancestry,
Num calligrafia / ki so bu tribo / peut reconnu and find secrets in,
That the world will read and try to listen to and bribe you to spill ...
Now, as you fly and look over your leather,
Do you see the paths that were once mere chemicals in the womb of your
 mother?
How 9 months formulated your armour into this,
An Arab-Creole tapestry worthy of being touched by the air that you
 breathe.
Your skin is like the land that you see from where your family reaps.
It sprouts protection.
You're –
A giver,
A nurturer,
A barrier of protection,
– Past, future, and present –
You sprout trees from follicles,
Create ecosystems and grow jungles,
– Enjoy that –
So you can be proud of what your future will reap.
Quite like the hair that you coil,
That, comes from the northern soil.
Eventually, Alchemists will turn to you to know how you have managed

    to make it exist like so –
Just remind them it is as simple as the existence of you from the womb to the world,
Juju that debunks the stereotype to the word.
It is not blackmagic.
To be of West African and Middle Eastern descent is *Black Magic*.
Endlessly affirming, effortlessly reminding of your badges of honour.

Tifany MarSah
Ode to red cedar wooden furniture

From their corners
To their textures
And colour,
I wonder
If they think of me in the same spectrum,
A member to their family instead of a stranger,
Imposter,
Or a mere object to mine.
Do they think of me in the same colour?
As in, Red Cedar,
(Guinea –) Bissau's soiled terra, Cabo Verde's eternal yellow-brown
    lumiere and Lebanon's Cedrus Libani,
The blend of every family member I've had the pleasure to be with, –
    in their presence,
A reminder,
That the sun isn't always so cold or so warm
And that Red Cedar may be the reason why I feel so at home
    away from home.
Red Cedar,
The colour of the soils in my *maternal* terras.
I wonder
If this familiarity is why I feel like I'm stepping into the warmth
    of something I haven't felt physically but rather *object'ively*
Thaw to my welcoming –
Red Cedar,
– My *maternal* cellar –
I really wonder
If all the travels we made to finally be together,
The ones that didn't necessarily 'wear and tear' the impeccability
    that is our exterior,
That brittled our interior,
Is why, I feel the heaviest clouds linger over the warmest place
    where I find your praise –
I wonder
If you'll ever escape my embrace,
Leave me to figure out the rest of my days
And force me to grow into the adult you've aided to raise,
But I collapse dehydrated to say,
*"Please don't fall for the chants of travellers and the bargains of easier
    lives for they will only burn my gaze and scald my site and soon be the*

reason why I sit here today to write this ode to your presence in my life."

Tifany MarSah
The Machine

My father isn't an exterminator. At least that's what my eyes say to me.
But when you work with the babylonians
A lot of secrets turn into the toxins you breathe
And just like for exterminators, death always seems to be a convenient
    toxin to fill up the streams,
You see ...
Before the mists of patriotism fell upon my family,
West Africa and Middle East armoured my birth
And my father personified the lever we'd pull to lather all my families
    pressures until the day I noticed his eyes blinking heavier.
Post workout rituals no longer served to strengthen.
Instead, the beds of his eyes comforted in red transparently opaque in anger
    or fatigue.
And I thought maybe this was the poison wanting to expose itself to me.
A painless vision began to invade his prism
And I guess you could say, it was all a matter of time
Before white matters became all that mattered to his day and soon mine too
I was baptised, the female version of my father's name, the reminder of my
    twinhood
His name, defining him, Generous and Honorable
And so in honour of his first name I began my generosity by sucking his
    poison until it began to spin in me –
I bit so hard into his veins he had to tattoo my face just to cover up the
    pain.
It wasn't enough to break him free though.
I let my eyes blur just like his.
After all, I am supposed to be the female version of him – right?
So I thought I'd also inherit the same side effects.
But even then, I just could never be this machine
– My father is able to camouflage in the pits of colonial acceptance,
Follow the outside quarters of Amilcar Cabral paths
And hide secrets in the lagoons and deserted streets to later come back
    to phone me and just sigh in relief to be in a bed where safety is found
    under his sheets.
My father's legacy falls on the hummingbirds to his daylight –
    the dream catchers to his –archy,
My brother – the Dreams, me – the Catcher with pockets big enough to
    capture
His pain, his trauma, his disappointment, his stress –
Because that's just what I was conditioned to be – a purifier
    – just not for me

No wonder this poison still runs through me – *and then they wonder why
I don't give blood –*
So many toxins it's hard for my liver to function how it should.
I became so engrossed in what stained my father's pain that I didn't realise how soiled I became.
Nonetheless, I don't regret a thing …
I pray, he never doubts, that when I leave the nest my main priority stands to detoxify my blood in faraway banks just so I can come back in enough time to drain any leakage he may have left before white matters can ever take care of the rest.

Epiphanie Mukasano
On The Move

I am a child on the move
plodding doggedly
on shaky ground

I am a chameleon
a child of many colours
a blend of many cultures

Amid blistering winds
I hold my grip tight
one foot at a time

I keep my head steady
turning my eyes in all directions
I don't want to lose my direction

I am a child of Africa
denied citizenship
I long to belong

I am a child on the move
a stranger to my extended family
an outsider to the table of humanity

I am from a place unknown to me
I am not from there
I am not from here

I hear there was a war
ravaging in my homeland
metallic machines spitting fire

We ran away carrying
nothing but seeds of hope
I was an infant then

Decades later
the suffering goes on
the seeds still fruitless

I am a child on the move

roaring like the Atlantic
digging up my fields of gold
I will make Africa proud

I am a child on the move
roaring like the Atlantic
I will dig up my fields of gold
I will make Africa proud

M Sahr Nouwah
Voyage of Freedom

My mama,
Embarking on a distant voyage of freedom,
Just eighteen, yet mother to two,
Left me with grandma.

My mama,
A tender heart of youthful years,
Journeyed beyond the Macona River to lands unknown,
In search of peace and love. What she had
Had long soured, turning life into a bitter grape.

But grandma saw hope,
Witnessed the fullness of God's grace.
No wonder she never gave up.

I am a twist of thorns,
Born to a young wanderer
On her long voyage of freedom,
Fleeing the chains of a bitter, broken marriage.

Today, I am a child of three nations,
The son of a wandering soul.
An orphaned heart, seeking freedom,
Shaped by life's cruel hand, yet still my mother's son.

In her sojourn, she found love,
Envied by the keepers of the land.
She found death in love's embrace,
Without a final goodbye.
Once more, she left me — this time forever,
Journeying to the afterworld.

In the woven fabric of fate,
Her journey lasted but a moment.
She found love but was battered by tears and death.
And I, left alone in a foreign land,
Sing a melancholic tune.

Before you left me, mama,
I learned that life weaves designs for us all.

Following your dreams,
I, too, now sail the voyage of freedom.

My mama, this is the voice of your shadow
Left on the battlefield of life.
A spell from your inspiration,
My mind stretches far beyond the oceans.
Here I stand — an immigrant,
Still tracing your path of freedom.

M Sahr Nouwah
Global Citizen

I am a refugee, they tell me.

But I am nation-less
With cravings, hopes and wishes
Jarring the power that owes me my rights.

I am a refugee, they tell me.

With rights and hopes.
My blood swirls.
My aspirations are never in a refuge.
Saving lives, building homes.
Still in service to this land.
Rejected and tagged.

I am a refugee, they tell me.

I sing for them.
I give them morning inspiration
In their offices.

I am engulfed and caged — holding on.

Today, I am the subway singer.
Tagged. Sharing my subway melody
In your closet.

Remember, my soul.

I ran from war.
I came home.

I am the rejected one
Famed and owned by my foes.

I am a global citizen. Call me that, and
I will smile like the morning star.

Cut my flesh, my blood is red. No tag.
Tear my heart, it is pure. No name.

I am not a refugee.
Do not call me names.

Call me a global citizen.
Make me home and see me proper.

I am a global citizen.
Staunch and bold.
I am strong and calm.
Lead me and I will lead others.
I am a global citizen.
Fearless.
My dreams are global
And my wishes will heal the world.
I dream humanity, not names.
I stand for solidarity beyond race, nation and religion.
I serve the good of *us* not just *me*
Whether you accept me or not.
I am a global citizen
Drenched in dreams of a world where
We are all one people.

M Sahr Nouwah
Migrant Promenade

Sitting before my shop,
Hungry and worried
And there, my thoughts are lightened.
And here I come on a promenade.

My feet chariots to the sound of the trumpet
To sojourn and to fend, all to make a name.
My African pride, melting in my bloodstream.
All in hopes for a better tomorrow.

Enduring the long-distance journey of the Sahel
And the long stays in the Kalahari Desert
All survived in the bosoms of hopes and dreams.
And for the helpers,
Only money makes sense to their ventures.
For us, the sojourners, we aim only to reach the promised land.

The noise is too much.
But we cannot hear.
The seas are rough but we venture
And they keep us hostage.
Yet, we will die trying.
And yet, we will die fending.

We are Africans.
Africa is the world.
We are the world.
Our colour is in every blood.
Every continent and every people, feel us.
Yet, they despise us.

But in the beauty of their cities
Lies the labour and sweat of our sacrifice.
Our wood is in every parliament.
Our gems are in every country.
We serve the world.
We sustain.
We are the world.

What they never write,
We are smuggled by them

To work their fields.
We earn them profits.
In their riches, they send home aids.
And we send home remittances.
All is money just enough to keep home safe and breathing.
Yet, no one celebrates us.

We are the Sojourners – the Migrants
We die on seas and fields.
Yet, we are uncounted.
But who knows this?
Except the news that serves only their interest.
But we are the World, even though we are not celebrated.

Mark Kennedy Nsereko
I'm ~~not~~ home

On a walk, I forgot I'm not home,
threw on a jacket to hide my crop top.
I'm wearing less eyeshadow.
I haven't outgrown being subtle.

At the café, I forgot I'm not home,
leaned back to dodge my boyfriend's kiss.
He thinks I'm ashamed of him.
I don't know how to love overtly.

In the club, I forgot I'm not home,
overthought my dance moves.
No one should see me twerking.

All I've known is hiding.

Mark Kennedy Nsereko
The Color Trials

I stand in the witness box,
mustering my color.
I clench my fists to summon the
color I've been suppressing forever.
I believe it's in there, somewhere.

I have to prove I am colorful
or they'll send me back
to where
        not being black or white
                                 is a crime.
To this court, colorful boys are pink.
I rue my blueness.

If I had known I would stand trial,
back at home, I would have forced myself
into high heels, wore wigs, painted my nails,
partied with flamboyant boys,
and left a trail of color
that may have have signed my death sentence.

I wish the judges of this court were Ugandan.
my people know how to spot a colorful,
right before they hurl stones at you.

How am I colorful enough to be
disowned, fired, and almost lynched,
but not colorful enough for asylum?

Mark Kennedy Nsereko
In Kakuma

He raises his sturdy black arms, their webs of veins bulge like they convey venom meant for me. They bulge from strength he has invoked to force the rock he carries into my scalp. His eyes boil with a scorn and aversion I don't understand. I thought he, of all people, would understand. We are in Kakuma Refugee Camp together. From different countries, – yes. He ran from war, I ran from hate; both wanted us dead. Yet, with conviction, he brings that rock down into me. I pray rainbows spill from my cracked skull to prove his belief that we are different.

Mark Kennedy Nsereko
In Utopia

a Zimbabwean journalist changes bed pans in a retirement home, babysits seniors all day and documents migrant plight at night;

a Ghanaian Master's student rehearses how to break it to their parents that they're staying behind to be their self; applied for asylum and won't return home;

a Ugandan bemoans not being erect in the sex tape he made with his boyfriend and submitted as evidence to the asylum tribunal; owing to no erection, the judge ruled he is not gay and denied him asylum;

a gorgeous Kenyan in a trench coat, with nothing underneath, walks into the hotel lobby, picks the presidential suite key card to go see the man who pays for his lifestyle;

a Nigerian cash cow wires half her pay cheque to Enugu, to the parents and siblings who disowned, battered and cursed her when she was caught with another woman.

Collins Chibunna Nwachukwu
Lost in Despair

Amidst plenty, the children cry
Dreams surrealistic highs
Pale and hay the skin, – toned grey
As though an open mortuary or at sea's eddying bay

Foundational, the curse,
Or a hand-made
Blistering aberration
Of a senseless
Numbing
Sense
The race of blessed discombobulated sages?

On lifesea, seamless and swaying.
Hopes sway on a thread, like uncertain pendulum tilts
And do we, like coins, toss deaths on high culminating tides
For a life born anew?

And from where did my skin go wrong
And how did my prime form foul
That in whimpering stammer, the name fizzles before our bewildering eyes
    as though 'Sizwe Banzi' in the enclave of the dying sun serrating
    rejuvenation

Hunger took them by the hand and promised them GRAVES
    in shallow roots,
    silence.
    Silence,
Still silence on arid desert aisles.
The boats weep blood, human blood.
The seas roar, and with it carry the children of dissidence

The sky bleeds now for you blacks
Steadied by pain, the tricky thorns of thwarted trails,
Silently.
And still, they let out the dog of neo-colonialism
And in our own coin we are paid, – no, they are paid!

Black race!
Frowned upon by passers-by
The skin, an appealingly dawning drowsy drop

From the heights of glory, to a passing diminuendo

We are heroes trampled by fate
Blemished by time of our passing dreams
Shrieking cries, – the skies weep blood
The rhythm of longevity dies in blackness

For so long we have wept sore
In starving hunger drills
These Mediterranean seagulls
Romancing the depth of the deep blue sea for the trove of treasures.
Raw gold in surfeit superfluity.

Yet we wail for the small fortune
For deaths came to us
Our progenitors the albatross, for they sold us out for few coins

Collins Chibunna Nwachukwu
Forced Marriage

Can two walk the miles except the souls meet as one
And for what use is a cistern, broken into smithereens,
Except for the dunghills

– So are these wayfaring men

In the cold freckled morning, freezing cold, and the hot sun simmering
– They to the line put life and limb
And on the dartful dizzying day, they line up, urchins?
And this amalgamation, black and white?

Over on the other side of the scorching deserts they come
Face to face with deaths in daggers drawn
All for the little little more

And the nights were mostly long, and the sea temperature, a death trap

Callous leaders, the earth's woes
For must they venture off to pastures so green
If at home
The songs are sweet?

Mirthless huts haunt us at silent nights of hunger
Eyes short with blood begging for few morsels

Earth is tired of despotism
Amidst much, the wealth of nations
Yet the race so small in prying eyes of white tones

Blessed race!
Yet glories shut out by hands so high in towers so cruel
That came as friends once, as soul-poachers, the last hope of despairing
    pairs, of ancestors cursed, and the day of perdition –

Hunger drove them from their hoes
Starvation stilled their rising dreams
And for desperation, they sold their souls
And the goddess of the seas smile at human calamities

The shores wash our ghostly bodies
The winds blow out our innards

The rhythm of pains plough on, heads on heads roll
And above the seas, over on the other side of the sea sand floats our future

Yet we might choose no amalgamation, with men who sold us for few guineas
For a hallowed name at heaven's gate, the hope of another heaven and pulled our resources ashore. Now we rush out madly, to tap from our immeasurable treasures

Arise Africa!
Up and awake, refuse this marriage forcefully proposed

Let the voices of the oppressed ring again
Let the lights shine now
For Africa is our home, and our garden of eden

Collins Chibunna Nwachukwu
Let Pan-Africanism Lead

If tomorrow comes by
Tell them they play on our intelligence
Tell them, the earth people conspire

For so long
They chanted our annihilation in their covens full of white witches and
    would not let us lie in our pastures green

For colouration
Above us they look
And esteem fairness over the COLOUR of the soil

But earth eats us all
There is so much division
The worms feast on our grumpy backs

Yet the lords hope for a cleansing
And when they talk of building
Destruction surfaces

Time is now we build our home
Now is time we roll as one
And ignite afresh our ancestral fire

For we look frail in comity of nations
Separating faces and skin
The idle works of perfidious foes

Skin lacerations
Tummies bloat
And man gloats, marries Beasts

Is this what you lure our Godly souls to feast
On food of idolatry and damnation?
But we stand again

For we are the urchins of earth's life

Helidah Ogude-Chambert
Knotted Bodies of Water

How do we map Black death?
      Black Afrika. Black Atlantic. Black Pacific. Black Mediterranean.
Time bends back upon itself. Stretching into the ongoingness of

ordinary atrocities.

For the Black (African),
time unfolds as violence. Again, in and through:
                        the violence-time unfolds…
                        layers of bodies. Spectacle

                        lynchings (as drownings)

How do we map the wounds that remain?
What crooked lines do these remains make…On the seabed, haunted by
   the silence of the dead.

                                  Knotted Bodies of Water.
Holding each other   (in something *other* than damage)

Helidah Ogude-Chambert
Strange Fish

He swam in the glare of the sun, in the **depths** of our **deep** blue sea.

                                                        Scrambling, heaving,

                                                                               sinking.

                                     Washed up.
They killed him. By the ships that abandon, in their *sea that swallows*.
                                Scrambling, heaving, gasping

                                …drifting…
Surrounded   by   strange fish

                                                           Washed up.
They killed them, I said. *All* of them.
In broad daylight, on sunny European beaches.
faceless.
     nameless. unnamed. ~~Nour~~
               forgettable. ~~Adama~~ forgotten.
               Unmournable.
They killed us, again.
                         And again.   Again.   Again.
                                     And again. And again.
Strange fish rotting in their sea.

Inspired by Giulia Bertoluzzi's documentary film, *Strange Fish*, Abel Meeropol and Billie Holiday's song, "Strange Fruit," and the many dead that the Waters remember.

Omobola Osamor
Searching for the Gap

I will take the 123rd Boulevard eastbound train,
get off at the last stop, walk up the steep 123-flight stairs,
three interspersed landings, each grimier than the companionway.
Walk past the archway with musty dark corners, floors noisily kissing
    dusty soles,
past the crosswalk with bamboo-bordered stalls,
the hobo holding a beaten cardboard sign, "Help me with a dollar,"
couldn't help but translate to naira, "Help me with N575."
The beach sand stretches—a grainy blanket carrying a motley crew of
    bodies,
prostrate, supine beet-red shins and torsos, hats atop sunglasses,
below some upright, some misshapen
flashlight–winking–coloured umbrellas and lopsided kiosks.
Another beach cuts to mind,
thousands of miles away—a cluster of lily-white pulsating limbed,
eyes squeezed shut, mouths open, "Halleluyah."
Agama lizard bopping heads, rending where blue meets sands.
I walk past the inhabitants of this till they are specks, and my calves ache
to claim my spot—without neighbours and footprints.
Gather seashells for a time.
Rolling waves crash, bubbles become effervescent,
foams infuse sand, soak the edges of ripped, once-black jeans,
salt assails tongue, stings nostrils, toes sink in mud,
the dwarf star sinks into the blankets of dusk, feathery breeze bestows
kisses, shore creeps closer,
grains of sand pinch my back, momentum gathering wind whistling the call
    of sirens,
waves' gentle tugs morph into jealous lovers.
Perhaps the brine would cleanse my pores of contrarian desires
my parents and pastor speak. *Make me clean.*
Restore that which was lost in the gap that brought me forth;
which bequeathed monthly bleeds and twin molds as breasts—the body of
    another.
In the gap—two souls switched places—each trespassing.
Somewhere, she searches for hers.
If the waves send me forth to where I jumped ship, will I recognize mine,
and will it be home, a glove—a second skin if I did?
Will it be a cage to a restless spirit?
Will it bear imprints of its former—sullied and bruised as she clawed;
swung edges of shards? Will it bear scars like mine,
wrists with half-moon beaded stitches, attempts to deconstruct who her

spirit says she is?
Perhaps I will have to break into it, develop bunions and corns—repair a leaking roof,
broken window panes and locks.
Will she find me? Will I find her?
In the gap.

Omobola Osamor
Following the Ancestor's Map to Freedom

A constellation of ancestors surrounds the smiling moon.

The sun cannot be trusted.
True, without her, maize withers,
She burns captive and free,
Sinks her teeth in fettered skin,
Leaves gravel on our tongues,
Fries us as we harvest cobs.

Thorn bushes cut my shins.

Onwards, the night is your friend.
We'll show you the path travelled,
Hide you like the cobra beneath palm fronds,
The scorpion at the river's fringes,
chicks beneath the mother hen;
you're safe in our blankets.

Moor stones graze my knees.

Left at the hibiscus trail,
beneath the palm trees,
gather fruits and eat.
Through the cobbled path,
tripping water downstream.
Stop. Quench your thirst.

Fear holds me in its steel embrace.

Those are our arms; keep moving;
Through the thicket,
At the river edge, mind that scorpion.
You won't drown; it's waist-deep;
Slather on mud, blend with the barks.

My friend is losing power to my foe.

Stay in the mangrove's shade,
It's cool within its embrace.
Be careful,
the adder has the same plans.

Sleep. You need your rest.

Adi's crying fills my ears.

The past drowned in the river bed.
When the cricket chorus halts
at the bitter leaf junction.
Freeborns aren't born and lost to fetters.
Swallow your tears, follow your friend.

Omobola Osamor
Home is

Ìmẹ̀ẹ̀kọ́ sitting within sacred groves,
resident in the shield of Ilé fe
from yonder plains.

Home is àkàrà pulsating in ogi,
láfún spread in welcome for ẹ̀gúsí;
it's wàrà littering teeth at noon.

Home is the call to prayer at dawn,
it's Mami travelling the labyrinth of sweat
beneath her burden of love,
knees black from kissing the altar.

Home is dew from her descent,
heavy in rosary garlands,
the dooring of tears within her wrappers,
the cocooning mint within her borders.

Home is where the mockingbird ceases,
and the queen of the savannah emerges,
the gathering of chicks beneath their mother,
it's the cooling within these walls.

Home is our oríkì igniting our paths,
the scuttling of adversaries beneath bejewelled nights,
it's gẹlẹdẹ masked ancestors dancing bọ̀lọ̀jọ̀,
the passing of the torch, from there to here.

Adaora Raji
Man hours

Tic tic tic
your clock is moving
because it is my perennially occurring lot
I must move with your clock

haul bags of cement to and fro the site
what else is my back made for?
Cement. Sand. Gravel
Mix.mix.mix
Mould.carry.plaster

my feet is aching
my back is breaking
my head is throbbing
but I must finish this
because a labourer deserves his wages

drill.drill.drill
drill till you bring forth black gold
then open the belly of the beast
in its belly you will find the blood of the innocents
it's breathing echoes the sound of mortars and warships
armageddon is now

mine.mine.mine
mine till you knock on hell's gate
the cavern spits forth fire but you must mine still
so that your master can adorn his women with the finest jewels

five fingers are not equal
you tell me
why do I have to be the small finger?

Adaora Raji
Mirror mirror on the wall

darling shiny mirror
faithful enough to grace us with your existence through the ages
we seek your validation once more
pray thee tell us who is the fairest?

is it she whose lips are full and luscious
or the other whose lips are light and taut?
behold our nasal ridges
should it point northwards or submerge between east and west?

are we to trade this brown fluffy halo for
long straight hair, straight like rice stalks in spring?
or we could do weaves, thousands of weaves that swing with our waists
straight. curly. ebony. blond. redhead.
you said what – scrape it all off

our skins are black like coffee
No – Brown. Freckled. Acne. Vitiligo.
yellow like pawpaw?
do you see how cellulite has drawn nature's tattoo from our hips to our
    thighs?
should our hips be weighty enough to gyrate to the drums
or just light enough to flow with ballet music in pointe shoes?

see how this bra strap helps to defy gravity
what size again – A. B. C. D. DD. Silicone
when do we free the nipple?

sweet sweet mirror
who do we crown the fairest?
is it he who can count his six to eight packs
and have eyes intense with passion that we burn with desire?
or the other with stomach muscles so fluffy that we can lay our heads
what length again – 4ft. 6ft. 8ft. 10ft
2inches. 4inches. 6inches. Phallus for sale

in many micro moments
mirror you lie because you do not see the inside inside
from that time when we threw our heads back with laughter
or that other time our chests erupted in a volcano of sorrows

and we resurrected from the mass tombs of stereotypes
into the new dawn of healthy confidence

Adaora Raji
we go where the grass is greener and the oceans are bluest

Land
We heard the grass is greener on the other side
so we poured libations to the ancestors
trekked with the fallow deer
buried our bones beneath the sands of the Sahara desert
and hung our hopes and dreams on the border fences of Melilla and Ceuta.

Water
We heard the waters are bluest on the southern shores
so we fled from famine and persecution
set sail on big ships
and filled our bellies with the fortune and freedom the Ottoman lands
    brought.

the other people cast nobility aside
set sail on even bigger ships and wandered off to new found lands
who would have thought that the human cargo criss-crossing the Atlantic
will lay the foundation for a New World Order?

we hear now the waters are bluest on the northern shores
when adelie penguins marched to the Antarctic convergence
we sailed on rickety boats through the Mediterranean
Sometimes we drowned, the other time we survived ten lives
to be rescued by coast guards
and built the eleventh life by the lagoons of Sicily and Malta.

Air
The arctic tern came to tell us of the existence of an extra terrestrial life
we want to see if that life is better than ours
so we flew in massive spaceships that soared to the moon.
melted our hearts in the centre of the Sun
and let the stars weave a crown around our heads
shall we hoist the flags now?
the aliens want to see our passports.

Fire
Preacher man says the after life is made up of two lands
and we must first lose this mass of flesh to journey into;
that land that is flowing with milk and honey
or journey to the other land of the dragon that breathes fire and hailstones
what Preacher man does not say is that
we must be purified first by fire to return again through water.

Laurène Southe
Fugitives of the Sun

Our parents were brought here by the ocean
And the moment their feet touched the ground,
Brick walls surrounded them.
With their bare hands, our parents
dug tunnels towards freedom,
Building homes out of alluvial soil
And roofs from leaves just like back in our homelands.
Despite all odds against them,
They bear promising children
Who carried on their eyes, lips and noses,
Calling us by names similar to their ancestors.
Soon enough, us children would
face their pain and be placed in cages
by the same people who built walls,
Calling us out of our names
For our parents were fugitives of the sun.
There are those who cursed at the wind
Who didn't blow our parents
off the fisherman's boat "back where you come from!"
Some tried to make amends with rain
Remind us all of our extended vertebral column
How all beings on the face of earth
must one day return to the sun.

Laurène Southe
Untitled

Lucky are those who can grow banana leaves with their own hands
Not for the beauty of it, but soon enough,
Fruits may crawl from its sweet air and fill the bellies of hungry infants.

Lucky are those who can make a shoe with just a single tool, which is patience.
To leave a trace of themselves in every footstep
Whilst decorating the surface of this world with its last human touch.

Lucky are the ones whose mothers carried their roof above her head
From treasures found in someone else's wasteland,
Only to see it stand stronger than any eighteenth century castle built from the back of slaves.
For it was drenched in heinous sweat and could not accommodate
Its guests without a culpable scent.

Unlucky are the ones who are forced to live with the mark of the devil:
Coltan smartphones and the silent tone of theft.
If they made it to the opposite corner of the world, it is because
They will never meet the eyes of her grievance,
Only to be avenged on the day of our deaths.

Laurène Southe
Mundele

There is this old saying of an African proverb,
It goes: "When an old man dies, a library burns to the ground"
And as an act of desperation, I'd fall on my hands and knees
Just to salve an inkling of hope from the ashes.
I never got to look through the pages of my grandparents,
Fill my empty stomach with their rich knowledge
For I was cursed with a foreign tongue
And feet so distant they could never reach their home ground.

CONTRIBUTORS

Abíọ́dún Abdul is a Yorùbá-Nigerian English Language Lecturer and UNESCO Global Poetry Slam Champion 2022. Her poems focusing on social justice and celebrating our common humanity are published in various anthologies. She also writes short stories, life essays and memoir-polemics exploring social issues encompassing her schooling across Yorùbá-Nigeria, Scots-Britain, and Japan. Book 1 is nearing publication and Book 2 is part of her PhD research. She writes/podcasts for literary magazines; performs at literary festivals/events; delivers writing workshops; and presents at academic conferences. Instagram: @abiodunoa

Nzingha Assata (nee Bedward/Gordon) is from Jamaica and has lived in England since January 1959. Nzingha is a mother, grandmother and great-grandmother holding a BA (Hons) in Social Science. She is also a retired health professional. As a community activist, she is a Garveyite, Pan-Afrikanist here in the UK, Jamaica and on the continent of Afrika. She takes her politics with her and aims to link with other activists when she travels.

Ayo Ayoola-Amale is the author of six volumes of poems. She believes that art expresses the inherent beauty in human experience and the environment with a sense of poetry and unbridled sensitivity. Ayo is a Social Justice Poet and the founder/director of Splendors of Dawn Poetry Foundation.

Jo Blackwood is an engaging and establishing street poet, writer, actress, community actress (Derby Theatre); (more recently) a digital online movie reviewer and hosts The Soothing Session (Derby Sound Community Radio Online). She has participated in development programmes, commissions, with Renaissance One London and volunteering programmes within the East Midlands community.

Efua Boadu. British-Ghanaian writer. In 2021, Efua was shortlisted to join the Southbank Poetry Collective. Her work has featured in Isele and Afritondo journals. She has been longlisted for the 2022 Afritondo Short Story Prize, the 2023 Mary Prince Award, and the 2024 Commonwealth Short Story Prize. Twitter/X handle: @FRH210.

Anayo Dioha is a lawyer and writer from the Igbo tribe of Nigeria. His poems lie on the online and print pages of The New Verse News, Queen's Quarterly, Password: Very Short Poetry and The Literary Cocktail Magazine. He's on course to complete a PhD in Law.

Philippa Hatendi-Louiceus was born in Zimbabwe and traversed three continents for education. Her journey culminated in a bachelor's degree in the arts. Scribbling since her teens, her pen dances to the rhythms of African culture, mythos, and folklore, weaving tales that honor the richness of her heritage.

Sierra Leone born artist and poet **Amanda Holiday** moved to the UK aged five. She has exhibited artworks at INIVA and Tate Britain and has shows forthcoming with Vivienne Roberts. Founder of Black Sunflowers Poetry Press, Holiday is currently completing a PhD in Poetry, Race and Art at Brighton University.

Sello Huma is a spirited and musically inclined poet and social entrepreneur from Limpopo in South Africa. His poems and songs are the books of our ancestors focusing on issues related to African unity, culture, history, futures and justice for people of color. Alongside his stage performances, his work can be found in the Sol Plaatjie European Union Poetry Anthology, Ons Klyntji, Afritondo, Agbowó, New Coin, Brittle Paper, Tampered Press and elsewhere.

Nandi Jola was born in Gqebera, South Africa. She holds a Master of Arts degree in English (Poetry) from Queen's University, Belfast, Northern Ireland. Nandi is a poet, storyteller, playwright and creative writing facilitator, and is well known in Northern Ireland and beyond for her work in the Arts and Museum and Heritage sector. Nandi was curator of the Golden Shovel Poetry Jukebox and is a creative writing facilitator for Quotidian. Among her plays, the topically titled *Partition*, and *The Rise of Maqoma*, engage with and also seek to move beyond Eurocentric themes. https://www.doirepress.com/writers/nandi-jola

Ilan Kelman is Professor of Disasters and Health at University College London, England and a Professor II at the University of Agder, Kristiansand, Norway. His overall research interest is linking disasters and health, integrating climate change into both. https://www.ilankelman.org/ and Instagram/Threads/X @ILANKELMAN

Tifany MarSah is an all rounded creative currently solidifying herself in the UK poetry scene. As a poet she encapsulates vulnerability through imagery, storytelling and conversation. Through "spoken letters" her pieces send a message from experience and paint a connection to past/present/ futuristic emotions and moments that are mutually experienced.

Epiphanie Mukasano was born in Rwanda in 1961. Now she lives in Cape Town and writes poems and short stories. Her poems were published in a collection, *Living on the Fence (2007)*, by refugee women from Africa. In 2010, she published her own collection, *Kilimanjaro on my lap*.

M Sahr Nouwah is a poet, humanitarian worker, and advocate with roots in Liberia, Sierra Leone, and Guinea. Born in 1984, and educated as a refugee, he has travelled widely across Europe, the Middle East, Asia, and the Pacific. Sahr writes articles on LinkedIn, Academia, and Medium, sharing his varied experiences.

Mark Kennedy Nsereko is a Muganda writer, and lawyer. His works are reflections on injustice. They are also glimpses into the orchestra of beautiful chaos that is his mind. These have been featured in the poetry anthology, *I Promise This Song Is Not About Politics* (East African Network of University Law Clinics, 2022), and in the magazines Brittle Paper, African Writer, Akpata Magazine, and Iskanchi Magazine.

Collins Chibunna Nwachukwu is a Nigerian and a Pan-African. Some of his works appear in anthologies that include *Love Birds* (Al-Lina Publications, 2024), *Words are Forever* (JET Publications, 2023), *Spirit Anthology* (a Radha Krishna publication, India), and *Achebe: The Soul Brother* (7th edition of the publication of the Young Society of Nigerian Writers, Anambra state chapter, Nigeria). Others appear in magazines such as Fringe Poetry Magazine (2024 edition, UK), and Mount Kenyan Times e-magazines (2023). A lover of music and musical instruments and a topnotch goalkeeper, Collins holds a BA in Mass Communication from the University of Nigeria Nsukka, and an MA in Communication and Language Arts from the University of Ibadan.

Helidah Ogude-Chambert is an interdisciplinary scholar-practitioner working at the intersection of migration/mobilities studies, armed conflict prevention, decolonial feminist thought, discourse, visuality, and affect studies, and race-critical theories. Her creative works are concerned with Black life, temporality, bodies of water, state practices of cruelty, everyday atrocities, embodied decoloniality and resistance. She holds a PhD from The New School in New York and is a Departmental Lecturer at Oxford University.

Omobola Osamor's poetry examines the intersection of relationships—both human and institutional—and the emotions that arise from failures and successes. Her work, which includes poetry and fiction, has been featured in a range of publications, including Brittle Paper, African Writer, The Shallow Tales Review, and Flash Fiction Magazine. Born and raised in Lagos, Nigeria, she currently lives in Chicago.

Adaora Raji's recent article for Salzburg Global Seminar explores how migrant fiction can challenge the narratives surrounding the complex global system of migration. Her fiction stories have appeared in Fictionable, Lolwe,

Arlington Literary Journal, Midnight and Indigo Literary Journal, the Coachella Review, the Bookends Review and as 1st runner up in the 2022 Kendeka Prize for African Literature.

Laurène Southe, a 24-year-old Congolese-Austrian writer, discovered her passion for poetry at 17 through the Vienna African Writers Club. Her full-time pursuit began after a 2021 performance at the African Diaspora Festival. She showcased her work in group exhibitions and at the Vienna Design Week, and completed her first poetry book, *Child of Congo*, during a writer residency at Echo Correspondence, aiming to publish it in coming years.

ACKNOWLEDGEMENTS

Some of the poems in this anthology have been published previously as follows –

"The Proud Afrikan", "I'm Saying That I Am Afrikan", and "Over the Horizon" by Nzingha Assata, in Nzingha Assata (1997). *In Praise of Our Ancestors*, Assata 1997

"Okukor" by Efua Boadu, in Afritondo, 22 May 2021. Available at <https://www.afritondo.com/afritondo/okukor> [accessed: 23 November 2024]

"Ode to the Four Market Days" by Anayo Dioha, in *Queen's Quarterly*, Spring Issue 2024 (pp. 144) under the title, "FOUR MARKET DAYS"

"Notes for a chronology of smell" by Amanda Holiday, in Anomaly (2020, Autumn Issue); shortlisted for Brunel International African Poetry Prize 2020

"Poem for Nesyamun" by Amanda Holiday, in Lolwe (2020). Available at <https://lolwe.org/two-poems-amanda-holiday/> [accessed: 23 November 2024]

"A Whiff of Something", by Amanda Holiday, in Anomaly (autumn issue) (US) 2020; shortlisted for Brunel International African Poetry Prize 2020

"African Icarus" by Amanda Holiday, in Issue 4, *Birmingham Literary Poetry Journal* 2020; shortlisted for Brunel International African Poetry Prize 2020

"An Ode to Makeba" by Sello Huma, in Afritondo, 30 April 2022. Available at <https://www.afritondo.com/afritondo/nbspan-ode-to-miriam-makeba> [accessed: 23 November 2024]

"The Crossroads spirits of the dead migrants must return home" by Sello Huma, in Tampered Press, December 2023 (blackness issue)

"The Dance", "Dear Belgium", and "The Great Migration" by Nandi Jola, in *New Hibernia Review/ Iris Éireannach Nua: A Quarterly Record of Irish Studies*, Volume 27, Number 1, Spring/Earrach 2023

"Strange Fish" by Helidah Ogude-Chambert, in H. Ogude-Chambert. (2023). What our Waters Remember: On Wasted Bodies as Strange Fish.

Border Criminologies blog. Oxford University, 10 October. Available at: https://blogs.law.ox.ac.uk/border-criminologies-blog/blog-post/2023/10/what-our-waters-remember-wasted-bodies-strange-fish [Accessed on: 18 October 2024]

"Searching for the Gap" by Omobola Osamor, in Brittle Paper, 30 January 2023

"Following the Ancestors' Map to Freedom" by Omobola Osamor, in Brittle Paper, 3 May 2023

"Home Is" by Omobola Osamor, in Brittle Paper, 28 August 2023

ORGANISERS

CivicLeicester is a community publisher that uses print and digital technologies, social media platforms, the arts, and online and in-person events to highlight conversations of transnational interest and significance. Books we have edited and published include *Black Lives Matter: Poems for a New World* (2023), *Poetry and Settled Status for All: An Anthology* (2022) and *Bollocks to Brexit: An Anthology of Poems and Short Fiction* (2019).

Forced Migration and The Arts is an international network that brings together people with lived experience of forced migration, refugee and non-refugee artists, academics and art spaces for conversation looking at work taking place at the intersection where forced migration and the arts meet. The network, initial stages of which were developed with support from the University of Manchester's Humanities Global Scholars Fund, hosts monthly indabas or discussion forums on the last Thursday of each month and encourages mutual support and collaboration: <https://forcedmigrationandthearts.blogspot.com/>

Regularise is a migrant-led collective founded in late 2019, prior to the COVID-19 pandemic. The collective aims to address the years of sustained hardships that undocumented migrants experience in the UK and continues to organise and campaign for justice and for the rights of undocumented migrants: < https://regularise.org/>

FINANCIAL SUPPORT

15 people pledged financial support for this project through our crowdfunder: <https://gofund.me/cf99e461>, enabling us to meet some of the costs associated with bringing the anthology out.

Black Lives Matter: Poems for a New World
Ed. Ambrose Musiyiwa

'*With over 100 contributions from writers of diverse ages and backgrounds, the collection is a poignant exploration of an era of renewed protest and newfound solidarities, against the backdrop of the coronavirus pandemic. [...] The revolutionary task of overturning imperialism cannot be achieved, the collection suggests, by appealing to those with power.* Black Lives Matter: Poems for a New World *urges its readers to take matters into our own hands if we truly want to build this new world.*' – Ananya Wilson-Bhattacharya, in *The Norwich Radical*

Poetry and Settled Status for All: An Anthology
Ed. Ambrose Musiyiwa

'*Poetry and Settled Status for All [...] consists of 114 poems by 97 writers from around the world. Introduced by Claudia Webbe, the MP (until recently, the Labour MP) for Leicester East, the book is a call for Settled Status or Indefinite Leave to Remain to be given to those with insecure or undocumented immigration status. Those who, as Diliana Stoyanova points out, are here already: "The rootless, the tongue-less, the restless, / The helpless, the aimless, the reckless, / The outcast, the voiceless, the faithless, / The exiled, the faceless, the state-less, / The immigrants, / The differents."*'
– Andy Croft, in *Morning Star*

Bollocks to Brexit: An Anthology of Poems and Short Fiction
Ed. Ambrose Musiyiwa

'*This is an anthology that wears its heart on its sleeve. Clad (perhaps not uncoincidentally) in Liberal Democrat yellow, it brings together an eclectic range of voices against Brexit, from established poets and spoken word performers to flash fiction writers and lyricists. [...] The contributors are motivated by feelings of sorrow, anger, frustration and alienation, and the anthology itself seems intended to offer a kind of therapy both to the authors and the presumed audience.*' – David Clarke, in *Sabotage Reviews*

www.ingramcontent.com/pod-product-compliance
Lightning Source LLC
Chambersburg PA
CBHW060205050426
42446CB00013B/2996